FOCUS ON THE FAMILY ®

HELP!
MY CHILD IS HOOKED ON VIDEO GAMES

HELP!
MY CHILD IS HOOKED ON VIDEO GAMES

dr. bill maier
general editor

Tyndale House Publishers, Inc.
Carol Stream, Illinois

A Focus on the Family book published by Tyndale House Publishers, Carol
Stream, Illinois 60188

TYNDALE and Tyndale's quill logo are registered trademarks of Tyndale House
Publishers, Inc.

All Scripture quotations, unless otherwise indicated, are taken from the *Holy
Bible, New International Version*®. NIV®. Copyright © 1973, 1978, 1984 by
International Bible Society. Used by permission of Zondervan Publishing
House. All rights reserved.

The case examples presented in this book are fictional composites. Any resemblance between these fictional characters and actual persons is coincidental.

The use of material from various Web sites does not imply endorsement of
those sites in their entirety.

Editor: Brandy Bruce
Cover photograph copyright © by Dimitri Vervitsiotis/Getty Images. All rights
reserved.

Library of Congress Cataloging-in-Publication Data
My child is hooked on video games / Bill Maier, general editor.
  p. cm. — (Help!)
"A Focus on the Family book."
Includes bibliographical references.
ISBN-13: 978-1-58997-173-8
ISBN-10: 1-58997-173-6
1. Video games and children. 2. Video gamers—Psychology. 3. Child rearing. I. Maier, Bill. II. Series: Help! (Carol Stream, Ill.)
HQ784.V53M92 2006
649'.64—dc22
                                    2006009217

Printed in the United States of America
1 2 3 4 5 6 7 8 9 / 11 10 09 08 07 06

Contents

Foreword

Addicted—it's a word we typically associate with things like drugs, alcohol, or gambling. But millions of parents in the U.S. are beginning to realize that their child may be addicted to something they *thought* was simply harmless fun.

These parents have confronted the painful reality that their son or daughter is spending countless hours each week glued to a video game console or a gaming Web site. They've noticed disturbing changes in their child's personality—their son seems obsessed with "reaching the next level" or their daughter's friendships are limited to the "virtual" world of an online gaming community.

If you're thinking: *That sounds just like*

my child, you've come to the right place. This book will provide you with the knowledge and information you need to help your child. We'll help you determine if your child's passion for video games is simply a passing fad or a serious problem that requires immediate intervention. We'll educate you on the disturbing link between violent video games and aggressive behavior. And if you do need to step in and take control, we'll give you solid recommendations on how to do it.

We pray that the Lord will guide you in this process and provide you with the strength and confidence you need to "stop the video-game madness!"

Dr. Bill Maier
Vice President, Psychologist in Residence
Focus on the Family

Game Wars: Three Tales from the Front

Amy tapped on her son Nathan's bedroom door, and then called out his name. There was no answer. She opened the door, and there sat Nathan, still wearing the same clothes as last night. His eyes were glazed over as he stared at the TV screen, thumbs frantically punching buttons on the wireless game controller.

"Five more minutes," Nathan demanded, his eyes glued to the game.

"You've been playing all morning. That's enough now."

"I just need five more minutes!"

Amy walked to the set and unplugged the game.

"No!" Nathan wailed. "I didn't save it!

Now I'll have to start all over! I hate you!" He threw himself on his bed and pounded his fists in fury.

Amy watched her 11-year-old son, speechless. He hadn't thrown a tantrum like this since he was two. What was wrong with him? It was just a game.

> ∽ ∽ ∽

It was a perfect Saturday afternoon. Joe went to find his son Sam in the hopes that they might have some father-son bonding time. He finally located Sam in the darkened basement. Sam wore a headset that blocked out all sound; he sat on the floor hunched over, fixing all his attention on the video game in play.

A tap on his shoulder broke the boy's trancelike concentration. "Hey, buddy," said Joe, "let's play catch."

It seemed to take a few seconds for the

words to register. Then Sam replied mechanically, "Sorry, Dad. I'm in a tournament here."

Joe sighed. "Can't you drop out?"

"They need me," said Sam, turning back to the screen.

"Okay," said Joe, trying to hide his disappointment. He noticed his teenager's shaggy hair, dropping below a frayed T-shirt collar. *When was Sam's last haircut?* Joe wondered. *Who are those kids he's playing with? And why do I suddenly feel like a stranger in my son's world?*

ꆤ ꆤ ꆤ

"Look!" said Anne. "Over there. It's a herd of antelope!" She twisted around in the van's front passenger seat to get the attention of the twins in the back. Both girls were engrossed in their handheld video games. "Quick! You'll miss it!"

"Miss what?" asked Molly. She slowly made eye contact with her mother.

"Look out the window! On Gina's side!"

By the time the two girls focused on the great outdoors, the antelope were far behind.

"When I was a kid, we liked to take family trips. But our kids get so bored unless they have their games. All they're seeing on our vacation is a two-inch screen!" Anne complained to her husband, Dave.

"Well, times have changed. At least they're being quiet and not fighting."

"Yeah," said Anne. But she wondered about it. The long drive did go more smoothly with video games, but at what price?

ᘯ ᘯ ᘯ

Do these stories sound familiar? Have you knocked on your child's bedroom door, only to find him or her engrossed in the latest video game? Have you experienced your child's fury over a game unplugged or the grief of an unsaved game lost forever? Does your child make time for video-gaming friends, but not for the family fun you used to share together? Do you wonder about the long-term impact of constant stimulation on young kids? Do you have nagging doubts about whether your child is addicted?

You're not alone.

Contemporary culture is rapidly changing, and kids today have a vast supply of entertainment choices. It's difficult for parents to keep up with everything that's available for kids ranging from toddlers to teens. From movies to music videos to CDs to iPods to the latest video or computer game, entertainment options are growing with emerging technology, and the video-game industry has quickly established itself as a major media outlet. In fact, combined sales of video-game hardware and software have already surpassed movies in gross sales.[1] And in a society where what's popular is constantly changing, parents struggle to stay informed in order to make good choices for their families.

The fact that you're reading this book is a sign that you're either hoping to derail a video-game addiction in your family or looking for help for someone who's already glued to the TV or computer. Are you hoping to discover that your child really doesn't have a serious problem, just a bad habit? In these pages, you should find guidance to help you identify how much of a problem video games are causing in your child's life.

Those dry, bloodshot eyes are not a good sign. Video-game addiction is real and something all parents should take seriously.

Most people consider addiction to be related to substances, mainly drugs or alcohol. But in reality, addiction can consist of anything that becomes such a priority to a person that he or she is willing to neglect friends, family, faith, responsibilities, and even physical health in order to pursue that priority. Electronic games have the potential for this sort of behavioral addiction.

Video and computer games have a profound influence on children in partic- ular because children retain more infor- mation if they learn actively, rather than passively.[2] Video and computer games are totally interactive, meaning that the child is actively engaged in what is happening on the screen. The addictive nature of video games will be explored in more depth later, but it's clear that they can cause problems in the same way that alcohol and drugs do.

In many cases, playing video games has overtaken people's lives. Gamers lose touch with reality. They push away friends and family because they are consumed with reaching the next level. They act irrationally and lose perspective, just like people with gambling or substance addictions.

As a responsible parent, you've chosen to get involved. In this short book we'll examine the facts about video games, offer suggestions for how to teach your child good habits and how to model good habits yourself, and provide pratical advice that will enable you to head off an addiction or break an unhealthy pattern that has already become established.

Developing moderation and self-control will change the way your child handles video games and promote new habits that will help him or her succeed in a variety of life situations. A helpful first step is to understand how video games have become so pervasive in today's popular culture.

What Makes
Video
Games So
Popular?

S teve Watters, author of *Internet Addictions*, wrote: "From the beginning, it seems, video games have been addictive. Whether they are guided by knobs, buttons, joysticks, or a computer mouse, they have beckoned users to escape into fantasy worlds populated by race cars, tanks, spaceships, mythical creatures, and more for the past 30 years."[3]

Just as movies and novels do, video games can provide an escape—a place to live out fantasies, to be someone else for just a little while. Video games go a step further because, through their interactive features, players feel involved and in control. Instead of watching a car race on TV, the player can be the one *driving* the car. Why watch a basketball game when you can choose to be any NBA player you want on a video game? With ever-improving technology today, video games can look almost lifelike, providing an authentic experience.

Video games are everywhere, in console or PC format. PC games are computer based, and many are available online. Computer games are as addictive as console-based video games, and both now offer online features, allowing for interaction with many players at any time of the day or night. Many games are portable, freeing kids to play while walking down the street or riding in the car. They punch buttons on handheld games such as Nintendo Game Boy Advance and Sony PlayStation Portable. Kids can play electronic games on cell phones and iPods. In 2004, sales of portable software game titles broke the $1 billion mark.[4]

The film industry has discovered the value of tying in with video games, and many major motion pictures are transformed into games. Peter Jackson, film director of the popular *Lord of the Rings* trilogy and *King Kong*, worked closely with Ubisoft to create the *King Kong* video game. Movie-based games like the handheld version of *Shrek* 2 are extremely popular with younger kids.

Video games such as *Resident Evil* (horror/adventure), *Lara Croft: Tomb Raider*, and *Final Fantasy* have been turned into major motion pictures. Television cartoons such as *Kim Possible* and toy characters including the popular *Bratz* dolls are now offered in handheld video game format. Even classic board games like *Sorry* and *Battleship* are now available as video games.

Just how big are they? According to the NPD Group, 2005 U.S. retail sales of video games, including console and portable hardware and software and accessories, were over \$10.5 billion.[5] Some of the "environments" (game worlds) are as big as medium-sized cities. Estimates of total gamers range from the tens of millions to hundreds of millions worldwide.

There is no doubt that this is a generation immersed in media. The average American child spends 44.5 hours a week in front of a screen, and 83 percent have a video-game console.[6] Many have several kinds of game systems, and this form of entertainment is growing steadily for both children and adults.

Because video games are so pervasive, parents need to be involved and informed. A useful parental tool is the Entertainment Software Rating Board (ESRB) rating system:

EC (early childhood). Content is suitable for ages three and up.

E (everyone). Content is suitable for ages six and up.

T (teen). Content is suitable for ages 13 and up. May contain mild language, violence, and sexually suggestive themes. Parents should use discretion.

M (mature). Identification required for purchase. Games rated M are sold only to gamers over the age of 17. Material in this category may include sexual themes, violence, and strong language.

AO (adults only). Identification required for purchase. These games are restricted to persons over 18 and are often sold only in specific game stores. Material may include graphic sexual scenes, strong language, and intense violence.[7] Seriously consider whether this material is appropriate even for you or your spouse.

Remember, as the parent you want to model good decision making to your children. In spite of the availability of ratings, 90 percent of teens say their parents "never" check the ratings before allowing them to buy or rent video games.[8]

Control is the key. The video-game phenomenon can add to your family's life if used in a controlled setting, or it can invade your home and take over the lives of vulnerable family members.

What Are the Dangers Inherent in Video Games?

Brian and Jenny were playing their new video game in the living room when Dad, casually reading the paper in the kitchen, overheard their conversation.

"You did that on purpose!" Jenny cried.

"Ha! You're too slow. You have to fight faster," Brian laughed.

Dad decided to move closer to see what the kids were playing. He settled into an easy chair and watched the game as they played. He recognized the open package on the coffee table, a birthday gift for Brian that had been at the top of his wish list. Dad's eyes widened as the character on the screen moved through crowds, holding a shotgun and shooting randomly. The character paused, pointed the gun at a victim's head, and pulled the trigger.

Dad's jaw dropped when he realized Brian was manipulating the character. Brian was the shooter! Dad grabbed the empty game case and quickly read the cautions, wishing he'd taken the time to do so earlier.

ɔ ɔ ɔ

A major concern is the increasingly violent and sexual content of video games.

Though not all games are bad, extreme caution is required. Some games are educational and just plain fun (with parental involvement and monitoring). But other games such as *Grand Theft Auto* that have a rating of M or worse celebrate brutality, violence, drugs, and even prostitution. In fact, *Grand Theft Auto: San Andreas* was originally released with an M rating, but was changed to AO after it was discovered that the game contained hidden sex scenes.

Even before this discovery, players could manipulate characters to have sex with prostitutes out of view, but unlocking this code allowed players to engage in a graphic sexual mini-game. The rating was changed to AO and stores such as Wal-Mart and Target pulled the game from their shelves.

Many M-rated games include first-person shooters, meaning the player is initiating the action. It becomes more personal than games where the player is just manipulating characters. In first-person games, the player himself acts out forms of violence. According to the American Psychological Association (APA), perpetrators of violence in video games go unpunished 73 percent of the time. Elizabeth Carll, cochair of the APA Committee on Violence in Video Games, states, "Showing violent acts without consequences teaches youth that violence is an effective means of resolving conflict. Whereas, seeing pain and suffering as a consequence can inhibit aggressive behavior."[9]

The National Institute on Media and the Family publishes an annual report that cautions parents on the top games containing sexual and violent graphics (www.mediafamily.org). In 2004, three of the top 10 video-game titles (ranked by sales) were *Grand Theft Auto: San Andreas*, *Halo*, and *Halo 2*.[10] Each of these games is rated M and has extreme violence.

While games like these are supposed to be off limits to children, their sheer popularity causes kids to find ways to access them. In fact, a 2004 study by the Federal Trade Commission found that 69 percent of young teens who tried to purchase M-rated games were successful.[11] And 78 percent of adolescent boys claim that an M-rated game is one of their favorites.[12]

In some cases, however, the government is getting involved. Governor Arnold Schwarzeneggar, Senator Hillary Rodham Clinton, and Senator Joseph Lieberman are among the politicians who have pursued legislation to restrict minors' access to M-rated games. Several states have attempted to pass legislation concerning minors' access to M-rated games; however, the free-speech argument has prevented many of these laws from going into effect.

Regardless of government involvement, or lack thereof, parents still have the responsibility when it comes to what's appropriate for their home. If you determine that your child already has a game that's too violent or graphic or contains questionable language, you have the right to take it away and forbid your child to play it. Be the parent, not your child's pal. Your child *needs* you to look out for his best interest.

New software permits parents to regulate computer-based video games using ratings systems. Sony and Microsoft have placed parental controls using ratings in their latest versions of PlayStation and

Xbox. Parental controls are also offered
on the online aspect of Xbox 360: Xbox
Live. These types of controls allow parents

9 9 9

After a series of school shootings, violent
video games drew special attention. Authori-
ties found that the shooters, almost without
exception, were big fans of point-and-shoot
games. That sparked debate over the games'
ability to fuel real-life hostility. Recent
research shows that playing violent games
can increase aggressive thoughts, feelings,
and behavior. Does that mean every guy
who plays Duke Nukem will turn into a cold-
blooded killer? No way. That's unrealistic.
But it would be equally foolish to pretend that
there's no risk from games that stimulate
endorphins, encourage brutality, and then
reward violence—a potent combination.[13]

to limit multiplayer options and filter downloads, but every family is different. The ESRB standards may not match your personal standards, so you still need to be actively involved in monitoring the entertainment outlets in your home.

Desensitizing Effects

According to online press releases from the APA, researchers at Saint Leo University found that after playing violent video games for a short period of time, young people experienced an increase in aggressive behavior.

One study showed participants who played a violent game for less than 10 minutes rate themselves with aggressive traits and aggressive actions shortly after playing.

In another study of over 600 8th

and 9th graders, the children who spent more time playing violent video games were rated by their teachers as more hostile than other children in the study. The children who played more violent video games had more arguments with authority figures and were more likely to be involved in physical altercations with other students. They also performed more poorly on academic tasks.[14]

Research has also found that boys tend to play video games for longer periods of time than girls. It's possible that because women are often portrayed in secondary and even degrading roles in video games, girls have less incentive to play.

Though there are documented cases of deaths that can be linked to excessive video-game playing, the most common danger is to a young person's emotional and spiritual health. Certainly any minor habit given the necessary elements can deepen into a dangerous addiction. Some gamers have claimed they are unable to break the hold video games have on them; the attraction to them is too strong.

If left unchecked, compulsive behavior can lead to serious problems. A parent needs to focus not only on the depth of a child's habit or addiction, but also on the underlying issue behind why video games have such a tight hold. The key question to ask is: What is driving my child to seek out these games? The answer might help determine whether or not your child is severely addicted to game playing.

Evaluating a Video-Game Addiction

What is commonly referred to as video-game addiction generally stems from two primary factors: internal rewards and social status. As with other addictions, there is a promise of getting something desirable back from the time invested—be it pleasure, power, alleviation of pain, love, or acceptance. Players are drawn into the games through the promise of return on investment. For some, it begins as the vicarious thrill of being another person. Gamers can live out their dreams in ways real life seldom, if ever, affords. A kid gets hooked on the fantasies because it fills a need to belong and be rewarded for his or her efforts.

Video games, online or otherwise, create a world that may be more appealing than life in the real world. Lonely, introverted people can feel a sense of power and accomplishment with each new level they reach. A person with insecurities might play a strong character, attaining a feeling of control. In other cases a player might take on a completely different persona—such as a man playing the role of a female character.

Three key areas where gamers find a payoff in their play consist of specific rewards, the approval of the gaming community, and physiological effects.

When a gamer completes a section of

⊙ ⊙ ⊙

"[Video-game addiction] is a huge and growing problem with older teenage males and young adult males. I've seen a number of cases with 17- or 18-year-old males where they have a broadband (Internet) connection and they basically haven't left the house for years."[15]

the game, he or she is instantly rewarded by reaching new levels, learning new skills, acquiring tools, and growing in status. Real life is much less certain; one often finds little or no reward for playing a hero. But by sitting at a computer, gamers can receive instant reassurance that their actions matter, for good and bad. With that instant reassurance comes immediate gratification. This factor attracts both children and also adults, who know that real life doesn't always work that way. It's a cleaned-up version of reality.

The online aspect of gaming presents an opportunity for a virtual society. Gamers can join groups that provide community and build a sense of accomplishment into the experience. These types of games provide a sense of belonging that many people don't have outside of the game. In the gaming world, status is achieved by how many hours a person has invested in the games. Many users attest that finding approval in gaming groups is one of the most compelling incentives to play the games. In fact, the acceptance of a community like this is filling an important need; but the fact that status is achieved through being the one with the most hours, rarest items, or highest addiction makes it unhealthy.

According to Daniel Sieberg of CNN:

Massively multiplayer online games, or MMOGs, saw their rise in popularity with the release of Sony Online's 'EverQuest' in 1999. For many, it was a chance to escape to a fantasy universe; to assume an alter ego and interact in a social network. . . .

Online gaming is seeing a surge in

popularity. According to the Entertainment Software Association, half of all Americans play video games—and 42 percent of them do so online. So far, it's attracted more men than women: Most online gamers—six out of 10—are male.[16]

In most online adventure/battle games, you win a challenge and your character grows stronger, allowing you to explore new parts of the interactive world. Many of these games bear a striking resemblance to the original Dungeons and Dragons role-playing game. While the elements may have changed, the concepts—identity, battles, rewards—remain the same. Essentially, the biggest change is that through computers, the scale has grown larger.

Hundreds (sometimes thousands) of gamers can be playing at any one time.

A player's network can range anywhere from a handful to several hundred fellow gamers, each with a unique identity that may or may not resemble them. "Flirting

---

ꝯ ꝯ ꝯ

I've heard parents bemoan the fact that kids don't get together anymore. The old knock on the door and request of "Can Timmy come out and play?" are now obsolete. My teens get together with their buddies frequently without even having to leave the house. They jump online with Xbox Live and instantly connect for a marathon game session. They use the game as a communication device, tuning in for the banter and updates even when they're not actually playing. These online games are quickly changing the face of childhood and adolescence.

—LIZ, MOTHER OF TWO

is another huge aspect with online games, since people can assume any personality and appearance they wish," says Daniel Sieberg. "With real-time chat, players can instantly communicate with friends or those they consider more than friends."[17]

There are times when the pressure from the online community becomes a factor in the reason why a child may feel the need to keep playing. A child may not want to "let down" his online group. If a child is playing because of peer pressure, he's no longer playing the game because it's fun. Especially for younger children, these online friendships can become valuable, causing a child to feel obligated to play even when he has other responsibilities.

Where can these virtual relationships lead? You might worry that the seemingly innocent friends your child is competing against online could be predators. Parental involvement is a must whenever children are interacting with strangers. These "friendships" should be closely monitored to avoid potentially dangerous situations.

Another key reason why video games are addictive is the physiological effect. Research has suggested that compulsive gaming may create an addiction response in the brain that is similar to a chemical dependency. According to an article in *Plugged In* magazine, "The root of bio-chemical addiction involves the same mechanism in all addicts: relying too heavily on one coping strategy to manage life. Addiction occurs over time when only one activity activates the brain's dopamine system, which instills a feeling of relief or well-being."[18] This feeling can give people an emotional high. And just like any other "high," the feeling has the potential to become addictive.

Four Signs of Addiction

There are a few telltale signs that indicate a potential video-game addiction. Certainly, if you're seeing any of the signs mentioned, it should be cause for concern. However, experts warn not to use the presence or absence of any of these signs, either alone or combined, as the basis for diagnosis. If you believe your child to be seriously addicted, you should seek the help of a professional counselor in your area. (For more information, or to locate a professional Christian counselor, call 1-800-A-FAMILY [1-800-232-6459].)

Sign 1: Blending Reality

A gamer says he got a good laugh when, after playing a particular espionage game for three days straight, he saw a security camera in a public place and froze. "It got me wondering," he says. "How often does stuff like this happen to gamers? Quite a bit is my guess."[19] Games can spill over into real life, for example, when a person

---

ෛ ෛ ෛ

My family and I were at the Air Force Thunderbirds air show last summer. We were treated to several flybys of current-day jets and WWII-era planes. The Thunderbirds team taxied by the crowd on their way out to the runway. What kid wouldn't want to stand within 50 feet of a team of F-16s as they thundered by? One kid with a Game-Boy. He was glued to the little screen, playing some game, as the real thing rolled by in front of him. His mom told him to put the game away. He answered, "Wait, I just have to finish this level."

—TOM, FATHER OF TWO

who has been playing racecar games for extended periods of time actually enters the real highway and those game instincts kick in.

Watch for behavioral signs of blending reality with fiction: using language picked up from a game, reacting the way a fictional character would react, talking only about a certain game, irritability when unable to play games—these actions and reactions could indicate that your child may be spending too much time plugged in.

Sign 2: Losing Sleep

Addicted gamers will often develop a pattern of giving up sleep to play video games. A gamer at any age can lose track of time when playing. Watch for signs that your child may be staying up late to play games. A child who shows signs of sleep deprivation, irritability, loss of appetite, is easily distracted, and lacks a desire for social engagement on a regular basis may be addicted.

Sleep deprivation can be a factor in a sudden change in grades as well. A child who stayed up half the night playing video games may be too tired during the school day to comprehend what is being taught. If you notice that your child's grades are slipping, he or she may be sacrificing study time as well as sleep time to play games.

Sign 3: Social Dysfunction

Griefer is the term widely used for online bullies or bully gamers. Emerging technology creates new ways for kids to bully each other. Just like bullies on the schoolyard, these kids who harass others online can cause emotional and social dysfunction. The problem for parents is that they may not even realize their child is being bullied. By talking openly and staying informed about who a child is playing with online, parents have a better chance of being aware when something is wrong. A child being bullied might become increasingly sullen, may choose to play the game only when no one else is around, suddenly have no interest in the game, or become depressed or edgy.

According to the Microsoft Web site, typical griefer behavior may include taunting beginners, using inappropriate or offensive language, cheating, forming virtual gangs with other griefers, or simply trying to annoy or harass a convenient target. Microsoft has posted tips for ways to deal with griefers on its Web site: http://www.microsoft.com/athome/security/children/griefers.mspx.

Another reflection of social dysfunction might be a sudden change in your child's activities. You may notice that he or she no longer wants to play with friends who aren't "plugged in" to video games. They may prefer staying home and playing games rather than going to the park or participating in outdoor sports.

Sign 4: Using Game Guides and Walkthroughs

Posted online to guide players through games, a *walkthrough* is essentially a map of the game that gives a player an advantage over other players. Particularly popular with massively multiplayer online games (MMOGs), players can "power-level" to higher status and earn the benefits of having played the game for dozens (sometimes hundreds) of hours in only a few minutes. This might sound like a good thing, since it may save time spent in a particular game.

But using these types of cheats to gain unfair advantage in a game can be a sign of a more serious problem, especially if the gamer is justifying the behavior regularly. Powerleveling not only cheats other gamers, it can also effectively rob the player of the simple enjoyment of playing the game, getting him or her more deeply addicted faster. With some online games, there are even well-developed characters for sale on gaming and Internet auction sites.

Quick Tips for Spotting Addiction

The patterns of pathological behavior have been studied by a group at McLean Hospital (Belmont, Massachusetts). Their findings with hundreds of video-game-addiction cases show that addicted gamers' lives are always significantly disrupted by the games. Some physical symptoms of addiction are also commonly present:

- Inability to stop the activity
- Neglecting family and friends
- Lying to employers and/or family about activities
- Problems with school or job
- Carpal tunnel syndrome
- Dry eyes
- Failure to attend to personal hygiene
- Sleep disturbances or changes in sleep patterns[20]

If you notice any of these signs in your child, take action. You may be wondering: *When should I intervene? Should I really be concerned?* Any of the above signs are an indication that your child is spending too much time in front of the screen. In cases of blending reality or using walkthroughs or cheat codes, you may need to just cut down on game usage. Increase time limits and actively monitor screen time.

If you fear your child is losing sleep or if you notice his grades slipping, you should remove the gaming equipment from his bedroom. Make sure the gaming console or computer is centrally located

9 9 9

"People tell me 'Hey, I'm not addicted. I only play a couple hours a day. The people you're talking about are on there all day and all night. I can control myself.' Well, in the couple of hours you take to immerse yourself in this virtual world, you are taking a couple of hours from your spouse or family. . . . Think about the amazing world you are missing."[21]

in the home and enforce time limits. If his grades continue to slip, you may need to remove the equipment from the home.

If you feel that your child's attitude and behavior have changed drastically—he or she is obsessed with the game and acts out with severe hostility when unable to play—you may need to seek professional help to discover possible underlying problems. This would relate to extreme situations. In most cases, gaming can be controlled with consistent enforcement of stricter rules.

There are many documented cases in which gaming has destroyed marriages, families, careers, and entire lives. Moms and dads have an opportunity to avoid those problems by noticing signs of addiction in their children early and taking action.

A good place to start is by logging

how much time your family is currently investing in media. Dr. Mary Manz Simon, author of *Trend-Savvy Parenting*, suggests setting notepads near the electronic areas in your home. Every time someone sits down at the computer, turns on the TV, or plugs into a video game, have that person mark down the time they spend at that specific media outlet. At the end of the week, count up the hours and examine whether or not you think too much time is being spent on media.[22]

Once the evaluation is done, it's possible for parents to step in and take action. That's not always easy in today's fast-paced culture, which promotes overwork and highly rushed lifestyles for busy families. But remember, you have the right and the responsibility to decide which games your child is allowed to play and how much game time is appropriate for your child.

Too many parents end up using video games as a babysitter to keep children entertained, not realizing that leaving a child in front of a screen for an extended amount of time can cause serious problems later. Other parents are in denial about the extent of the problem, rationalizing that "it's just a game" or "the game provides an outlet for aggression; I'd rather my kid play a violent game than act out violence in real life."

As the problems from video-game saturation become more evident, parents who haven't set up preventive measures find themselves doing damage control. Let's look at specific steps that might head off problems before they begin.

Part
Three

Practical
Steps to
Take Control

Mary and John were frustrated. They'd found their son, Mike, playing video games past bedtime again. His grades were failing. He often lied, promising Mary and John that he didn't have homework so he could play his video games. Mary had suggested throwing away the games, but Mike's pleading and tears and promises had held her back. Their once outgoing, active son now preferred to sit in front of the television set for hours, playing video games with online friends, trading real life for a growing addiction.

9 9 9

Maybe your child has just entered the world of video games, and you are concerned about the amount of time he or she is investing in this new virtual fantasyland. Or maybe you're worried about the kinds of games your child is playing.

It's vital that parents take the time to find out what kind of entertainment is influencing their family. If you're going to allow video games in the home, be involved in the buying process. Below are a few helpful reminders when purchasing video games:

1. *Always check ratings.*

Reading the ratings is a good start, but as seen with games such as *Grand Theft Auto,* the video-game-industry rating system is not infallible when it comes to determining what content is appropriate for families. And despite the rating, sometimes there are "cheat codes" that players can hack into that could possibly alter the content. No matter what the rating on the package says, parents should research the material to ensure that the content is appropriate for their family.

2. *Read expert reviews and consult other parents.*

Take the time to research games that your child wants to play. Read online reviews. Al Menconi Ministries offers video-game reviews at www.almenconi.com. *Plugged In* magazine by Focus on the Family offers one review of a popular video game per issue, or visit pluggedinonline.com. Videogametrouble.org has good advice for moms and dads concerned about video games. Exchange knowledge about games with other parents. This can help parents decide whether to pursue a game with their children, or avoid the game once they realize that the material is not suitable.

3. *Rent or borrow video games before buying.*

Video games can be very expensive, and game consoles are even more costly. Before plunking down the money for a high-priced game, try borrowing the game from the library, renting it from a game-rental outlet, or even borrowing a game from a friend. Some stores sell previously owned games. Check return policies and trade-in possibilities before purchasing a game.

4. Set time limits and gaming rules for your family.

Before gaming, set clear time limits and rules. Mom and Dad should decide what the time limits and rules will be. Remember to be consistent with enforcing those limits and rules. As the parent, you have the right to decide what games are allowed into your family's home. You might want to set parental controls if your gaming console or computer game has that option.

5. Try the game yourself or take time to watch your child play.

Playing video games with your child, or at least watching your child play a game, gives you firsthand knowledge of the content. Try renting a few multi-player games and letting the whole family get involved. Even just watching your child play can provide teachable moments. Your child will be more likely to talk about the game with you if you're aware of what the game is about.

Breaking an Addiction

Whether your child's interest is simply fun and games or something more serious, for many video-game lovers, gaming is not the problem. If you believe your child is looking to the game for a better life, ask yourself what is it you hope to achieve by intervening.

Are you willing to spend more time with him or her? Psychologists agree that it is when the addicted person believes he can find acceptance, love, and approval apart from the video game that the pattern of addiction is easiest to break. Experts also agree that the best solution for most

---

🎵 🎵 🎵

My six-year-old son had a 45-minute fit when I took away his brand-new Star Wars computer game. Fortunately it was still in the shrink-wrap so I could return it.

"But Mom," he protested, "Star Wars is okay for games. I have another one!"

I hugged him and answered, "I know, but that one is a game about building droids. This one is different. It's rated T."

"Then why did Grandma buy it?" he said. "Didn't she know?"

addiction cases is to gradually increase
the amount of time spent with the child,
while gradually decreasing time spent in
the video world. In some cases, video-
game addiction is serious enough to war-
rant professional counseling assistance.

Remember that each case is different,

Ͽ Ͽ Ͽ

The problem was that Grandma didn't know
that games have ratings. All she did was go
to Wal-Mart to select a game that she
thought her grandson would enjoy. There
was nothing on the cover to suggest the content was overtly violent, except the "T" rating.

"We'll have to tell Grandma about the
rules at our house. I'm sure she'd like to
take you back to the store and find one that
will be more fun."

—MARIANNE, MOTHER OF THREE

just as every child is different. One parent said that he had tried everything to break his son's gaming habit, and finally had to physically remove the equipment from the home. Surprisingly, his son expressed more relief than anger. He had been unable to stop playing on his own.[23]

If your child is playing video games several hours each week and you think that he or she is addicted, you may need to remove the equipment from your home. This situation would relate to children who have lost contact with friends and family members, have seen a decline in their school grades, and are unhappy unless plugged into a video game.

However, simply enforcing stricter house rules may work for other families. Try keeping electronic equipment in central locations rather than a child's bedroom. That approach can not only help parents keep track of how much time is being spent playing video games, but also improve a parent's ability to monitor closely what games are being played.

Authors Olivia Bruner and Vicki Caruana give excellent advice on how to control the gaming experience for your children:

- Set time limits.
- Make sure all chores and homework are completed before play.
- Be intimately involved in choosing the games your children play.
- Remember—you are the grown-up! Model good viewing and gaming habits yourself.
- Suspend play if you see that your child is having difficulty with self-control.
- Monitor attitudes and behaviors with your child when he plays with friends or siblings.

- Encourage your child's friends to play at your house.
- Watch for signs of addiction to video game play, particularly with boys.[24]

How Much Time Is Appropriate?

There's no standard for how much time your child should spend on a video game each day. Neither is there a standard for how much time you should spend one-on-one with your child. Simply making the decision to be intentional about monitoring how much time your child spends glued to a computer or TV screen is a good first step. You know your child's strengths and weaknesses best. You decide how much gaming time is appropriate for him or her and hold to that standard.

However, today's generation of children is being introduced to media at very young ages. Some software is even directed at toddlers. The American Academy of Pediatrics (AAP) recommends that children under the age of two should not have screen time.[25] Keep in mind that the younger your child is, the more vulnerable he or she is. Children under the age of eight still struggle with separating fantasy from reality. Exposure to violence will have a stronger effect on these children.

It's a good idea to decide beforehand what your expectations are for your child's gaming experience. Mom and Dad should decide together what they deem is an acceptable amount of screen time. Talk together about rewards and consequences and boundaries and limits. Pray for wisdom and discernment. Parents should present a united front when setting house rules for gaming, especially in the case of

A tool that has helped remove us parents from the unpopular role of "game police" is called the Time Scout. My husband and I set a certain number of weekly hours the boys are allowed to play, and these hours are logged into a machine connected to the video-game system. The boys have cards (that look like credit cards) to swipe in order to turn the system off and on. Once their time is used up, they can't play any more that week.

Losing game time has also become a useful consequence of bad behavior, and it's easy to implement with the Time Scout technology.

—BETH, MOTHER OF TWO

divorce when parents may have different rules.

Then before giving your children a new game, explain clearly how much time they are allowed to spend playing the game and what the consequences will be if they choose to go over that limit. Mom and Dad should clarify that they always have veto power concerning what games are appropriate and access to the child's game collection. Rules will vary with different families, but by setting boundaries at the beginning, your child will know what you expect from him or her and what is unacceptable.

Building Strong Communication

Communication can help you understand why your child is attracted to a certain type of media. If your child is hooked on a certain game or begging for a new type of equipment, take that opportunity to talk about it together. Opening the doors of communication benefits both you and your child. By talking openly about video games or other types of entertainment, you are showing your child that you are interested in what he or she is doing. By knowing what new game is popular, you can dig deeper into real reasons why this game is attractive and why your child is interested.

Maybe you aren't sure what questions to ask, or you're afraid your child will be defensive and resist talking together. The following media discussion starters should help. These are general questions you can use to discuss all forms of media with your child.

- What is it about this form of entertainment that attracts you? Why do you like this particular style (or

genre or show or game) more than
the others?

- Why do you listen to, watch, or
play this? (If it's simply because
friends do, ask, "Why do your
friends listen to, watch, or play it?")

- How does this form of entertainment make you feel?

- Do the ideas reflect reality? Do
they reflect truth? If they reflect
reality, do they also gloss over evil
or enhance it?

- How do the messages conveyed
compare with the values you've
been taught at home or in church?

- Do you think these messages have
any effect on how close you feel to
your family, friends, or God? Why
or why not?

- Does this entertainment reflect an
opinion about God? What is it?

- What would happen if you imitated the lifestyles and choices of the characters in this game or this program?
- What do you think is inappropriate entertainment? Where do you draw the line?
- How does it make you feel to know that by purchasing a CD, going to a movie, or buying a video game, you are supporting the ideas being promoted?[26]

Spending time with your child away from the screens is a key factor in helping break the grasp of video games on your home. We've seen that kids look to video games and online players for immediate acceptance into a virtual world. So what can you do?

Provide alternatives. Instead of just insisting that your child stop playing video games, choose an activity that the two of you can do together. Replace gaming time with face time. Shoot hoops, read a book, or bake cookies together.

Another way to avoid the potential for a gaming addiction is to model self-control techniques. Set aside one hour to watch a program together. Be intentional about turning off the TV when the program is over instead of flipping through channels. Make a date to spend half an hour playing a new video game together. Designate a specific time to start and end. Be prompt about turning off the game when the allotted time is over.

For some gamers, the online gaming community is a draw, but others prefer to be isolated, playing alone. Take notice if the only friends your child talks about are those he has met in the gaming community. Playing video games shouldn't take the place of physical activities that provide stimulation and healthy movement. Keep in mind that media can play a factor in childhood obesity.

Of course, this extreme doesn't apply to all situations; but all children do need physical activity to remain healthy and strong. You can look for video games that require activity (some games teach dance steps and require movement), but if your child is simply spending too much time in front of a screen, provide other alternatives such as play dates, trips to the park, a family game of basketball, or even a simple bike ride through the neighborhood.

Games attract parents for many of the same reasons that they attract children. A stay-at-home mom may enjoy the community feeling she finds in online video gaming. A dad whose real life—work, family, bills—seems mundane or stressful might find relief in entering a fantasy world where he can feel rewarded for his accomplishments.

Sometimes a love of gaming is actually passed down through the parents. A dad who loves to play video games will share that with his kids. While there is nothing wrong with parents and kids enjoying games together, keep in mind that this is a great opportunity for moms and dads to display good gaming techniques. You can teach self-control by stopping the game in an appropriate time frame, having a good attitude whether you win or lose, and concentrating on having fun instead of getting ahead.

Focus on the Family receives many letters from parents who are concerned for their children on a number of issues, including video-game usage. This letter was sent to Bob Waliszewski, director for Focus on the Family's *Plugged In* magazine:

Dear Bob,
My son is very interested in violent
video games. He defends them by saying
it's the "fight between good and evil—
and, Mom, I'm always on the side of
good!" I'm not sure how to respond to
that. Can you help?

Here's Bob's response:

Many parents who operate from the
axiom "Pick your battles carefully"
make the mistake of viewing video
gaming (and negative entertainment
in general) as a lesser skirmish best
ignored. I, however, believe differently
for a number of reasons. "Violent
video games are not games of fun,"
explains retired Army Lt. Col. David
Grossman. "These are mass-murder
simulators." Likewise, Iowa State Uni-

versity psychology professor Craig
Anderson is convinced violent video
games increase aggressive behavior
and thinking. "One of the great myths
is that unrealistic violence has no
impact," says Anderson. Not surprisingly, nearly every school shooter was
a fan of violent video games. And
although most players aren't tempted
to commit murder, I do believe there's
a more subtle desensitization occurring
in the hearts of many. Chris Taylor, a
staff writer for *Time* and a regular
game reviewer, explains how he strug-
gled getting *Quake III* out of his mind.
"I'd play it, then walk out into the
office corridor and realize I was looking at my coworkers as potential tar-
gets," explained Taylor. "I was so used
to killing anything that moved."

Another reason to set healthy

guidelines in your home regarding the Xbox and PlayStation is that according to a study by the National Institute on Media and the Family, one in seven gamers is addicted. Of course, gaming obsession goes well beyond the violence issue, and underscores our need to set time limits on even the most innocent games.

Furthermore, although your son rationalizes the violence by claiming to be on the side of "good," many of the M-rated games have a number of other problems besides the blood and gore. Sexual themes and profane language (often with hardcore rap music accompanying) are frequent. I'd suggest helping your teen find healthy game alternatives (they're out there), then set a time limit.[27]

Balancing Faith and Video Games

It's true that many families have decided that the positive aspects of gaming are heavily outweighed by the negative effects. However, for those families who choose to allow video games into the home, a balanced approach can make all the difference.

Consider content: What is your child learning from this game? Not every game has to teach a lesson, but almost assuredly your child will learn something from any game you choose. This doesn't have to be a bad thing. Gaming can improve hand/eye coordination. Games can teach reasoning skills and even life-application skills. Family gaming can provide interaction between parents and children. Showing an interest in the games your child loves can help develop your relationship with each other.

Do the research together. Find fun or

educational games that you can all play, and then model good fiscal judgment by borrowing, renting, or shopping for used games. Look for teachable moments when playing. Talk about how the characters interacted: the decisions they made, how things could have been done differently, and how those aspects of the game might relate to people of faith.

You might wonder: *What does Scripture say about video games?* Philippians 4:8 states, "Whatever is true, whatever is noble, whatever is right, whatever is pure, whatever is lovely, whatever is admirable—if anything is excellent or praiseworthy—think about such things."

Psalm 11:5 warns of the dangers of loving violence.

According to Proverbs 4:23, we are to guard our heart, for "it is the wellspring of life."

What can we learn from these verses? God cares about what we allow into our hearts and minds. As parents, you are the gatekeepers of what comes into your home. It's like a healthy diet: What you put into your body will affect how you live. By giving your child fruits and vegetables and making sure he or she gets plenty of exercise, you are contributing to a healthy body.

The same goes for what we put into our hearts and minds. By giving each of your children positive experiences, you are contributing to a healthy mental, emotional, and spiritual life. Invest in positive influences for your child.

In the end, your child's love of video games is not bad in and of itself. Yet left alone in that world long enough, he or she will reap the consequences of out-of-control use. Ultimately, it is up to you.

Your choice to intercede in your child's life—to set and enforce guidelines—will make all the difference.

Give it time. Be vigilant. And don't give up.

Notes

1. Katie Dean, "Academics Can Be Fun and Games," Wired News (www.wired.com), November 13, 2003.
2. "Video Game Addiction and Video Game Violence," The Parent Report Radio Show, http://theparentreport.com/resources/ages/early_school/behavior/1766.html.
3. Steve Watters, *Overcoming Internet Addictions* (Ann Arbor, Mich.: Vine Books, 2001), 54.
4. "The NPD Group Reports Annual 2004 U.S. Video Game Industry Retail Sales," NPD Group, January 18, 2005, http://www.npd.com/dynamic/releases/press_050119.html.
5. "The NPD Group Reports Annual 2005 U.S. Video Game Industry Retail Sales," NPD Group, January 17, 2006, http://www.npd.com/dynamic/releases/press_060117.html.
6. "MediaWise® Video and Computer Game Report Card/A Ten Year Overview," The National Institute on Media and the Family, http://www.mediafamily.org/research/report_10yr_overview.shtml.

7. "ESRB Game Ratings," Game Rating and Descriptor Guide, http://www.esrb.com/esrbratings_guide.asp.

8. David Walsh, et al., National Institute on Media and the Family, "Interactive Violence and Children," Statement to the Committee on Commerce, Science, and Transportation, United States Senate, March 21, 2000.

9. "APA Calls for Reduction of Violence in Interactive Media Used by Children and Adolescents," APA Online Press Releases, August 17, 2005, http://www.apa.org/releases/videoviolence05.html.

10. "The NPD Group Reports Annual 2004 U.S. Video Game Industry Retail Sales," NPD Group, January 18, 2005, http://www.npd.com/dynamic/releases/press_050119.html.

11. "Marketing Violent Entertainment to Children," Federal Trade Commission, July 2004, pdfversion available at:http://www.ftc.gov/bcp/workshops/violence/.

12. David Walsh, et al., National Institute on Media and the Family, "Ninth Annual MediaWise Video Game Report Card," November 23, 2004.

13. Michael Ross, *Boom: A Guy's Guide to Growing Up* (Carol Stream, Ill.: Tyndale House Publishers, Focus on the Family, 2003), 176.

14. "Review of Research Shows that Playing Violent Video Games Can Heighten Aggression," APA Online Press Releases, August 19, 2005, http://www.apa.org/releases/violentvideoC05.html.

15. David Becker, "When Games Stop Being Fun," IDC, as reported by IDC, an independent research firm in C|Net News, April 12, 2002, http://news.com.com/2100-1040-881673.html.

16. Daniel Sieberg, "Confessions From an Online World," CNN.com, November 3, 2005, http:// www.cnn.com/2005/TECH/internet/06/23/gaming.first.person/.

17. Daniel Sieberg, "Confessions From an Online World," CNN.com, November 3, 2005, http:// www.cnn.com/2005/TECH/internet/06/23/gaming.first.person/.

18. "Addicted to Video Games," *Plugged In*, January 2006, 2.

19. "Have you ever . . ." The Bearer, Zoned In Column, GameZone.com, http://ps2.gamezone.com/news/05_23_04_05_03PM.htm.

20. Maressa Hecht Orzack, "Computer Addiction Services," adapted from www.computeraddiction.com.

21. Alex "Epic" Blonski, "Online Gaming Addiction," RPGPlanet Editorials, February

5, 2000, http://www.rpgplanet.com/features/
editorials/addict/ (accessed February 10,
2006).

22. Dr. Mary Manz Simon, *Trend-Savvy Parenting*
(Carol Stream, Ill.: Tyndale House Publish-
ers/Focus on the Family, 2006), 134-135.

23. "Computer Game Addiction," Berkeley Parents Network online, http://parents.berkeley.
edu/advice/teens/gameaddiction.html.

24. Olivia Bruner and Vicki Caruana, "How to
Control the Experience," http://www.focus
onyourchild.com/entertain/art1/A0000803
.html.

25. "Television and the Family," American Academy of Pediatrics, http://www.aap.org/family/
tv1.htm.

26. Joe White and Jim Weidman, adapted from
the *Parent's Guide to Spiritual Mentoring of
Teens* (Carol Stream, Ill.: Tyndale House
Publishers/Focus on the Family, 2001),
342-343.

27. Bob Waliszewski, taken from the *Focus on
the Family* magazine, June 2005, 27.

Dr. Bill Maier is Focus on the Family's vice president and psychologist in residence. Dr. Maier received his master's and doctoral degrees from the Rosemead School of Psychology at Biola University in La Mirada, California. A child and family psychologist, Dr. Maier hosts the national "Weekend Magazine" radio program and the "Family Minute with Dr. Bill Maier." He also acts as a media spokesperson for Focus on the Family on a variety of family-related issues. He and his wife, Lisa, have been married for more than seven years and have two children.

FOCUS ON THE FAMILY®

Welcome to the family!

Whether you purchased this book, borrowed it, or received it as a gift, we're glad you're reading it. It's just one of the many helpful, encouraging, and biblically based resources produced by Focus on the Family for people in all stages of life.

Focus began in 1977 with the vision of one man, Dr. James Dobson, a licensed psychologist and author of numerous best-selling books on marriage, parenting, and family. Alarmed by the societal, political, and economic pressures that were threatening the existence of the American family, Dr. Dobson founded Focus on the Family with one employee and a once-a-week radio broadcast aired on 36 stations.

Now an international organization reaching millions of people daily, Focus on the Family is dedicated to preserving values and strengthening and encouraging families through the life-changing message of Jesus Christ.

- -

Focus on the Family Magazines

These faith-building, character-developing publications address the interests, issues, concerns, and challenges faced by every member of your family from preschool through the senior years.

Citizen®	*Clubhouse Jr.™*	*Clubhouse™*	*Breakaway®*	*Brio®*	*Brio & Beyond®*	*Plugged In®*
Focus on the Family Citizen® U.S. news issues	Focus on the Family Clubhouse Jr.™ Ages 4 to 8	Focus on the Family Clubhouse™ Ages 8 to 12	Breakaway® Teen guys	Brio® Teen girls 12 to 16	Brio & Beyond® Teen girls 16 to 19	Plugged In® Reviews movies, music, TV

> **FOR MORE INFORMATION**

Online:
Log on to www.family.org
In Canada, log on to
www.focusonthefamily.ca

Phone:
Call toll free: (800) A-FAMILY
In Canada, call toll free:
(800) 661-9800